ALLEGRA CHAPMAN

Creativity is your self-care

52 creative therapy exercises to support your emotional wellbeing all year round

For Pete, Chloe and Noah.

Contents

Introduction

This is a matter of life

You are a creative soul - that's what led you here.

You yearn to write, draw, paint, make things with your hands, express yourself in one, or several, of a million different possible ways to show who you are and what you feel through creative means, but you've been holding yourself back and suppressing your soul's creative longings.

You have been conditioned to believe that creativity is a luxury. That it is frivolous or childish or pretentious. That it is for "proper artists", not for mere mortals; only the super-talented chosen ones should spend time on it. You have been taught that you have more important things to focus on, that you need to concentrate on being busy and productive in ways that serve the system more effectively.

Well, I am so glad you're here because I have important news - creativity is vital to your wellbeing. You are a creative being on a creative planet. Just look at how the Earth creates new and varied life every single day. Look at the stunning colour palette that nature paints with. Humans have been making art and telling stories from the earliest moments of our existence - it is who we are.

You are a creator.

You need creativity. It is necessary for your emotional, mental and even physical health. You might not be surprised to hear that creative activities (from writing and drawing to gardening and sewing) have been found to reduce stress and anxiety, release endorphins in the brain to increase happiness and reduce depression, help you process difficult emotions and improve self-esteem. But did you know that creativity can also boost your immune system, lower your blood pressure, increase cognitive function and reduce inflammation that can cause chronic pain? It also helps to guard against dementia and maintain good motor function as you age.

Don't let anyone tell you that creativity is a luxury that you don't deserve. It is central to your wellbeing.

Creativity is your self-care.

Hello!

My name is Allegra Chapman. I am a writer, author, columnist and creative wellbeing practitioner. I'm also an amateur artist and photographer who loves to knit and bake. I'm not necessarily that great at most of those last things - my skills are definitely with words - but I love them and they bring me joy.

I am passionate about the power of creativity for wellbeing, and about helping people to unleash their creative spirit and express themselves in a way that feels joyful.

If that sounds like your kind of vibe, you can join my community, The Gathering, on Substack. There, I share regular creative exercises to support emotional wellbeing, I hold live online creative wellbeing workshops, and I share writing on creativity, mental health, neurodivergence and parenting. Find me at gathertogether.substack.com

How to use this book

This book is intended to help you discover creativity as a self-care practice.

There are 52 exercises - one for every week of the year. I know it can be hard to set aside time in your busy life for creative activities, but, as you've seen, it will benefit you massively if you do. Time spent supporting your wellbeing means you'll have more energy, motivation and staying power for everything else you want to give time to. So I highly recommend dedicating a space in your schedule each week to your creative self-care.

These exercises are intended to be simple and straightforward - easy to pick up without needing loads of experience and expertise in a particular field, or any expensive materials. They are gentle introductions to the kinds of activity that can be beneficial to your emotional wellbeing. As you find the types of activity that you most enjoy and you become more confident in your creative practice, you can take a deeper approach with exercises that will explore your needs and challenges in more detail. If you join my community on Substack, we work on these together each month.

Planning time

Setting a regular time each week that's planned into your calendar will make you more likely to stick with your practice, and helps it to become a regular habit. The trouble with most self-care activities is that we start off with good intentions, but then life intrudes and, before we know it, it's been weeks, then

3

months, since we did anything to nourish ourselves.

I invite you to put time in your schedule, right now, that will be non-negotiable every week. It only needs to be 15 or 20 minutes, if that's all you can spare (although longer would be better!). But block it out, every week, and stick to it. That time is sacred. It is time to nurture the core of who you are, and all other elements in your life will benefit from it, I promise you.

If your life, or your needs, are unpredictable, then it's ok if sometimes you can't make that creative date with yourself or if you need to shift it around in your schedule. The last thing you want is for your creative practice to become a source of anxiety or guilt. By trying to plan regular time, we're doing our best to build a regular habit, but sometimes life is just going to life and we're going to have to go with it.

You can take the exercises one at a time as your allotted self-care time comes around each week, or you can flick through and choose one that calls to you in the moment.

Materials

At the beginning of each exercise, there will be a list of supplies you need - I've tried to keep this as simple as possible so that you won't need to buy a load of art products, but there might be some items you want to get in or get ready ahead of time. I suggest that, each week, you take a look at the next exercise you plan to do a day or two ahead of time so that you can prepare anything you need.

Some general materials that will be useful for many of the exercises:

· A pad of A3 paper (for most exercises, A4 will do, but larger

4

paper will often work better)
- A notebook or journal (I'll let you into a secret - a journal is just a notebook, you don't need anything fancy)
- A pencil
- A pen
- Crayons
- Paints
- PVA or decoupage glue

Look after yourself

Your wellbeing comes first at all times. If any of the exercises trigger difficult feelings or emotions, only you can be the judge of whether you want to keep working through them and continue with the exercise, or whether it is better for your mental health to put the exercise aside. If you are feeling emotionally fragile on the day you come to your creative practice, you may be best looking for an exercise that will be gentle for you.

Sometimes working through difficult feelings through creativity can be beneficial, but don't push yourself to work with anything that doesn't feel ok to you.

When tough feelings come up, if you want to carry on with the exercise (or if you want to take a moment to decide whether to carry on or not), take a moment to focus on your breath. Place one hand on your heart, one hand on your belly. Close your eyes. Breathe in deeply through your nose, feeling your belly and your ribs expand. Breathe in for a count of 5, hold your breath for a count of 5, then exhale slowly through your mouth for a count of 5, and hold for 5. Then repeat this cycle a few times until you feel calm.

If you find, after the exercise, that you are struggling to deal

5

with anything that has come up, please do seek mental health support.

Any time that you are having a hard time with your mental wellbeing, reach out for help. In the UK, reach out to your GP for an NHS referral, or directly to a private therapy provider. The Samaritans offer free and confidential listening support online or by calling 116 123. If the situation is urgent, you can contact NHS 111, who have a dedicated mental health service. In an emergency, always call 999.

Outside the UK, similar urgent care and emergency options will be available – an internet search will usually tell you the relevant details.

We see a doctor or other relevant professional when our physical health needs a lift, we should always do the same for our mental health. Please look after yourself, always.

Enjoy!

I hope that this selection gives you an opportunity to experience a few different creative techniques that you might not have tried before. Maybe you'll fall back in love with an activity you used to enjoy, or allow yourself to unleash a passion for a particular practice that you've been feeling you have to stifle.

More than anything, I hope this book helps you to lay the foundations for a regular creative practice that brings you joy and wellness. You are a creative soul, and your soul deserves to sing.

1

Seeing Beauty

What you need:

- A camera (a smartphone is perfectly fine)

The world can sometimes feel like a lot. Regularly seeking out beauty helps to lift our spirits, and also reminds us that beauty is all around us. We live on a magical planet and, however difficult life gets and however much pain there is, there is still so much to be amazed by and to enjoy.

Exercise

Go out for a walk. Look for things that are beautiful. They can be natural elements - trees, flowers, the sea - or man-made objects. They could be things that aren't typically considered beautiful, but that you find beauty in.

If going outside absolutely isn't an option, find things of beauty around your home or the space you are in.

Take it further

For a more advanced version of this exercise, take a selection of your favourite photos from the first stage and display them either somewhere in your home or online (if you put them on Instagram or Substack, do tag me so I can cheer you on - I'm @allegra_chapman on Instagram / Threads and @allegrachapman on Substack).

Alternatively, make a collage from the images or draw your own pictures inspired by them.

2

Memory Journaling

What you need:

- A journal / notebook or some paper
- Something to write with

Journaling is probably one of the best known and most popular creative wellbeing exercises. But many people think that it has to involve writing an account of your day every evening – it can be that, if that's what you enjoy, but it doesn't have to be at all.

Journaling doesn't have to be daily – it can be weekly, or monthly, or just whenever you feel like it. It can involve writing about something that's happened to you recently, or years ago, or something that you want to happen or that you're worried about happening. Or you can write about a feeling, or an idea, you can write a letter to yourself or someone else (you'll never actually show it to them) or to an emotion... Journaling can take whatever form you want.

Exercise

Write whatever comes into your mind when you see the following sentence:

These are the things that I want to remember.

3

Blackout Poetry

What you need:

- A piece of writing (from a book, magazine or other publication, or printed from the internet)
- A black pen OR black paint
- **Optional:** Any other art materials (paints, pastels, crayons, you name it)

You might think that poetry is hard or complicated, but it's just a collection of words. All you have to do is choose some words and put them one after the other. And if you're worried about finding the right words yourself, why not start with someone else's? Using existing writing to create your own releases some of the pressure and self-criticism we can feel about writing, but it's also an interesting challenge because we can't use whatever words we want - we're constrained by what's already on the page. This can push us to come up with new ideas and connections that we wouldn't otherwise have thought of.

Exercise

Take a piece of writing. You can pull a page out of a book, if that doesn't go against your beliefs. You can also use a page from a magazine, a newspaper, a piece of junk mail... anything with words on will do. Alternatively, you can find a poem, a piece of prose or even a famous speech online and print it out.

Then use your black pen or paint to black out some of the words, leaving only selected ones visible. The words you leave visible form a new poem. You might start by choosing one or two words that jump out at you as interesting or unusual, and then see what you can find to follow on from there. Or you might start with an idea in mind and try to see if you can find the words to fit. Just start choosing words, and see where they take you.

Top tip: I like to go through the text and draw a box around my chosen words in pencil first. This means I can read through a few times and see if I want to make any changes before I commit, and also helps me to identify where I need the black ink/paint to stop so I don't accidentally black out a word I wanted to use.

A quick note on sources: As this is just for you, it doesn't matter what text you use. Copyright rules do not apply to private work. However, if you are going to make the piece you produce public, and enough of the original text is visible to make it recognisable, you may need to obtain permission from the copyright holder.

4

Self-Portrait

What you need:

- A piece of paper (I recommend A3 size, but A4 will do)
- A pencil
- Crayons / pastels / paints / anything you can use to make colour
- **Optional:** Collage materials

We're going to create a self-portrait, but don't worry - you don't have to be a great artist for this. This is nothing to do with creating a picture that looks like you, and all about helping you to lean into what makes you *you*.

Exercise

Draw an outline of a head. It can be as detailed as you like - it could just be a circle with some shapes inside for eyes, a nose and a mouth if you want; or, if drawing is your bag, you could go to town and make it look just like you.

Now draw inside the head images, shapes or colours that represent things that matter to you. If you're using collage materials, you could also stick in anything that feels symbolic to you. For example, when I did this exercise I used a segment of a book page and some sheet music; I also drew in flowers to represent nature and hearts to represent my family.

Around the outside, draw/ paint/ stick images, colours and/or shapes that symbolise spaces that are important to you and key parts of your personality. Amongst other things, I used paint to represent the sea (I'm obsessed with the beach and the ocean) and fire (I can be both highly passionate and a bit hot-headed).

Keep adding anything that you can think of that represents the essence of who you are. Don't label things as "good" or "bad", and don't put anything that you feel "should" be there - just allow yourself to bring together all the elements of your authentic self.

Take it further

If you want to extend this exercise, once your picture is finished, you could spend some time journaling on what this brought up for you and what makes you who you are.

You could also think about any elements of your personality that you see in the picture that you don't completely love, and identify what's good about them. (For example, my hotheadedness has certainly caused me some trouble, but it also helps me to be good at standing up for what I believe in and to prevent myself from being pushed around.)

5

Gratitude Collage

What you need:

- A notebook / journal or small piece of paper
- A larger piece of paper (A3 is preferable, A4 will do)
- Something to write with
- Glue or washi tape (you could also use sellotape)
- Magazines / brochures or anything you can cut images out of
- And/or an internet connection and a printer
- And/or more paper and something to draw / paint with

Gratitude has been proven to have a range of health benefits - not only supporting a positive mood and helping to manage depression and anxiety, but improving sleep, boosting resilience and supporting the immune system. Studies suggest gratitude can even reduce chronic pain and lessen the risk of heart disease. So worth getting involved with then!

Exercise

Use your notebook or small piece of paper to make a list of between 10 and 30 things that you feel grateful for. These can be as big (family members, friends, some major good luck you've had) or as small (sunshine at the window in the morning, flowers by the side of the road) as you like.

Don't spend too long on this - you might want to set a timer for five minutes and just get down as many things as you can think of in that time. Don't pressure yourself to put down things you think you "should" feel grateful for; search your heart for the things that inspire a genuine feeling of joy and pleasure, that make the world seem a little bit better.

Once you have your list, you're going to find (or make) some images that represent some of the items.

- If you're using magazines, brochures and other similar materials, flick through them and see what pictures catch your eye and feel connected to any of the items on your list. They don't have to be exact representations of the items, as long as they make sense *to you*. For example, if your gratitude list includes "how comfortable my bed is", you might spot a picture of a cosy blanket or fluffy cushions that make you think of that sense of comfort. If you have "the flowers I pass on my way to work" on your list, you don't need to find an image of the exact type of flowers or flowers in the right context - a picture of a vase of flowers could do the job. Or even an image of a colourful abstract painting could conjure up the same experience of vivid colour that inspires your sense of joy.
- If you're taking images from the internet, a similar ap-

17

proach applies, but you can, of course, be more specific in your search terms. Don't worry about copyright on images - this is just for you so you can use whatever you want. Just be aware that if you were going to display your finished artwork anywhere public then you **would** need to make sure that any images you used were in the public domain (for example by using a free stock image site like Unsplash or Pexels). Once you've found images you like, print them out.

· Alternatively, you could make the images yourself by drawing or painting them.

You don't have to find an image for every item on your list. Again you might want to set a timer for 20 minutes or so and gather as many images as you can in that time. Otherwise you might find yourself overthinking it and getting frustrated that you can't find the perfect picture, and that's not what this is about.

Once you have your images, take your large piece of paper and stick your images to it in whatever arrangement feels good to you.

You could also decorate your collage with paint, drawings or written words if you like.

You might like to display your finished collage somewhere in your home to remind you of all the things that make you feel gratitude every time you see it - helping to support all those health benefits we looked at earlier!

6

Feel the Rhythm

What you need:

- Enough space to move around
- Something you can play music on

One of the best ways to get your creativity flowing is to get your *energy* moving. Putting music on and moving your body lets you get out of your head and connect to your physical self. You can listen more deeply to your gut feelings, your inner knowing. You can also shake away stress, be present in the moment, get your heart rate up and support your all-round physical health.

Dancing to drum music is also said to help you tune in to the rhythm of the Earth itself. It's a primal sound that humans have been making for thousands of years, and one that we can easily lose ourselves in. I love Japanese taiko drumming - there is something almost hypnotic about it.

Exercise

You don't need a huge space as you can keep your movements as small or as big as your room will allow, but make sure the floor is clear of anything you could trip over or bump into.

Then put the music on and just allow your body to move in whatever way feels good. You can search for "taiko drumming" (or another form of drum music if you prefer) on YouTube or any music service and find a whole load of options, but here's one I found earlier: https://tinyurl.com/5aah87x3

Try to keep going for 15 - 30 minutes.

Please only do what feels comfortable and reasonable for your body. If dancing is out of the question, you can just sit or lie with your eyes closed and listen to the music. See what images, colours or ideas come into your mind during this time. You could then draw, paint or journal on what came to you.

7

Letter From the Future

What you need:

- Paper
- Something to write with

Sometimes we can get so caught up in our current stresses and worries about the future, that we forget that many of the things we're worrying about will either never happen or will have been forgotten about in a few years. Looking at our lives now from a long-term viewpoint helps to give us a little perspective.

Exercise

Write a letter to yourself now from yourself in 20 years' time. Imagine what that future version of you would want to tell current you. What lessons will they have learned that they want you to know about? What new perception do they have of the things you are struggling with or hoping for now? What words of support and encouragement would they want to give you?

Take it further

You could post the letter to you, and then save it to read in a few weeks or months.

You could even write it as an email to yourself, then schedule it to be sent in six months' time so that you receive an email from the future when you've forgotten all about it.

8

Free Drawing

What you need:

- Paper
- Pencil
- **Optional:** crayons, pastels, paint sticks or other materials you can use to make colour

One of the biggest barriers to building a regular creative practice that will nourish us and support our wellbeing is getting hung up on whether we're "good" enough. I'm here to tell you that there is no "good" in art - it's all personal, it's all subjective, and you are entitled to express yourself in whatever medium feels good to you. You don't need anyone's permission, and you don't need any qualifications.

That said, I know that pesky inner critic can be hard to shake off. So this exercise is good practice in letting go of any worries you might have about perfection and any desire to control the outcome.

Exercise

Spread your paper out on the table. Take your pencil (or crayon, pastel... whatever you like) in your non-dominant hand (so if you're usually right-handed, use your left hand). Start moving your pencil (or whatever) across the paper. Don't worry about what it looks like - this is your non-dominant hand; of *course* it's not going to look perfect.

If you're using a variety of colours, change colour whenever it feels right to do so.

Don't worry about what you're drawing or creating, just allow yourself the freedom of making marks on the paper without worrying about whether they're "right".

When you're getting used to the discomfort of using your non-dominant hand, try closing your eyes while you continue to draw. With your eyes closed, you could try switching between hands. Try to find the edges of the paper with your hands so you can fill as much of the white space as possible.

Take if further

An extension to this exercise is to use paint. If you do this, make sure you're wearing clothes that you don't mind getting messy, and that whatever surface you are painting on is also covered to protect it. Because this *does* get messy.

You could do the basic version of this exercise first as a warm-up, then get a fresh piece of paper.

Have whatever you want to paint with (brushes, sponges, etc.)

within reach. Put pots of paint out in front of you for easy access (or you can just squirt dollops straight onto the paper), and close your eyes. Then just go for it. Reach out for whatever brush/sponge/etc. and whichever colour your hand finds, and move it across the paper in whatever way feels good. You could even just use your hands to apply the paint. Find the edges of the paper with your fingers so that you can be sure you're covering every bit of white space.

When you think you're finished, keep going for a bit longer.

See what you can create when you're not trying to control the outcome.

9

Emotions Map

What you need:

- Two pieces of paper (A4 or bigger works best)
- Paints, pastels or something that you can use to make large shapes in different colours
- A pen or pencil

So often in life, we bounce around from one emotional state to the other, feeling that our lives are happening *to* us and that we're powerless in the face of it all. This exercise gives you an opportunity to take a step back and think about what situations trigger different emotions within you. What fosters joy, what stresses you out, how you feel at your best and your worst, and how you can nurture the former and reduce the latter. By mapping your internal landscape, you gain a better understanding of yourself and you can consciously cultivate a life that works a little more *for* you.

26

Exercise

With the first piece of paper in front of you, think about recent times that you have felt angry, frustrated and stressed.

Feel where those emotions sit in your body. Close your eyes, and try to visualise the emotions - what colours, shapes, maybe movement can you see?

Take your paints, pastels or whatever medium you have chosen, and depict the colours and shapes of those emotions on your piece of paper.

Put that piece of paper to one side, and take your second piece.

Now think about recent times that you have felt joyful, fulfilled and energised. Again, feel where those emotions sit in your body. Close your eyes and try to visualise these. Then depict them on your piece of paper.

If you've been using paint or similar, you'll need to wait for it to dry. This might be a good opportunity to go for a little walk, or do something that feels comforting and nourishing to you (curl up with a book, make a cup of tea, do some deep breathing). Anything that will relax your nervous system and ground you back in the present after dealing with those different emotions.

Once your paint is dry, take your pen or pencil. On your first piece of paper, write or draw the incidents or thoughts that led to you feeling angry, frustrated and stressed. While you're doing this, think about what it was about those incidents or thoughts that gave you that feeling.

Then take your second piece of paper, and write or draw the incidents or thoughts that led to you feeling joyful, fulfilled and energised. Reflect on what it was about those incidents or thoughts that gave you that feeling.

Now look at those two pieces of paper. You have in front of you a map of your route to joy and your route to stress.

Spend some time journaling on what you can do to bring more joy into your life, and what you can do to try to reduce the stress (or at least help you manage the stressful experiences).

10

Finding Freedom

What you need:

- A notebook or some paper
- A pen
- A pencil

Freedom is one of those things that most of us say we want, but few of us truly know how to achieve, or even how to define. And of course, we can't get to it if we don't know what it is. This exercise is an opportunity to think about what freedom means to you, and what it would look like in your life, so that you can consciously work towards cultivating that feeling.

Exercise

What symbolises freedom to you? Try to visualise a few abstract concepts that represent the idea of being, or becoming, free. A few suggestions to get you started: a key, an open door, a bird flying high... Spend a few minutes making your own list.

Now choose one image that feels the most powerful to you and draw it in the centre of a piece of paper.

Around that picture, write down things, situations, experiences that make you feel free or that would give you a sense of freedom in your life.

While you're thinking of what to write, you could doodle other images that represent freedom around the edges of your paper, or draw images to represent the things you've already written down.

Once you've written as many as you can think of, feel free to decorate your page in any way you like.

Spend some time journaling on which of the things you wrote are possible right now and how you can have more of them in your life, and which you need to work towards and how you can do that.

Keep your image as a reminder of what freedom means to you.

11

Homemade Instruments

What you need:

This exercise is about using things you already have lying around. So raid your recycling and your cupboards and see if you have any of the following:

- Saucepan or tin cans and wooden spoon
- Plastic bottle and rice, lentils or dried beans
- Cardboard box and rubber bands
- Glass bottles and/or drinking glasses and water

We've seen already that music and movement are good for our health, and another thing that's incredibly valuable for wellbeing is *play*. As adults, we've largely forgotten how to do it, but if we can re-learn to play and let ourselves go in the moment, it will not only reduce stress and anxiety, but will improve creativity, boost problem-solving and cognitive function skills, and even improve physical health.

Exercise

Using whatever items you can find, make some musical instruments.

If you want to keep it simple, a saucepan and/or some tin cans make great drums when hit with a wooden spoon. You can also fill an empty, dry plastic bottle with dried rice, lentils or beans to make a shaker.

If you're feeling more adventurous, cut a hole in the centre of one side of a cardboard box (or use something like a tissue box that already has a hole in one side) and put rubber bands over the box so the go right around the box, crossing over the hole. You've just made your own guitar.

You can also fill a selection of drinking glasses, or glass bottles, with varying levels of water - when you blow across the top, they will make different notes, a bit like pan pipes.

When you've got your instruments, let yourself get lost in making some improvised music!

12

Glimmer-scape

What you need:

- A notebook or some paper
- Something to write with
- Bigger paper (A3 ideally, A4 will do)
- Pencil / crayons / pastels / charcoal
- If you're planning ahead, take a notebook and pen with you all week so that you can note down the "glimmers" you'll be using for this exercise - but if you don't have chance to prepare in advance, that's fine

This helps you to focus on the "glimmers" in life. Glimmers are the opposite of triggers. They're the little moments of joy that pop up in the midst of the everyday. We are programmed to focus on the stressors and the perceived threats in our awareness because this is how our brains seek to keep us safe. But, over time, continual focus on negative or challenging things can wear away at our mental health.

We can't ignore the difficult parts of life, but, by bringing more awareness to the positive, bright spots as they occur amongst the challenges, we can become more resilient and optimistic in the face of whatever life throws at us.

Exercise

If you are able to plan ahead, make a note of any glimmers as they occur throughout this week - any moments when you feel a burst of joy, see something beautiful, experience kindness, are shown love, or are awed by nature.

If you're coming to this exercise with limited time and haven't been able to plan ahead, simply reflect over the week that's just gone and write down as many glimmers as you can remember from the last seven days.

Once you have your list, take your larger piece of paper. Draw images that represent those glimmers. They can be literal pictures or more abstract interpretations, it's up to you. Try to link the pictures in some way - either by using similar elements in two drawings, or by using shapes or patterns to connect them. Decorate them in any way you like.

You could display your finished picture somewhere to remind you of the little moments of joy that life has to offer.

13

Imprint Your Future

What you need:

- A piece of paper (must be bigger than your hand)
- A pencil

Some cultures believe that your hand is an extension of your heart, and so printing your hand onto the page is symbolic of setting down your heart. When you make images or writing with your handprint, you are therefore making a commitment to the emotions, needs and beliefs in your heart. Even if you don't believe this, using your body in your creative work is a powerful way to engage your whole self and tap into deep senses of knowing and feeling that we often dismiss in our modern world.

Exercise

Put your hand onto the piece of paper, and draw around it.

In the image of your hand on the paper, in each of the four fingers, write one thing you would like to achieve in the coming months. Choose the timeline to suit you - if there are a lot of changes you're looking to make, the next three months might be enough. If you have more long-term projects to work on, you might want to make it six months. I would recommend not making it more than six, as life can change so much so quickly that 12-month timelines can quickly become unmanageable - if you've got something you're working towards in a very long-term way, maybe think about what you *can* achieve in the shorter term that will contribute to your bigger goal.

"Achievements" don't have to be big, and they don't have to be about getting anything or about external validation. You might want to achieve a slower pace of life or a greater sense of calm. You might want to achieve less reliance on consumerism or eating fewer animal products. It doesn't have to be a promotion at work or writing a book.

If you're an overachiever by nature, you might have to do some thinking to narrow it down to four priorities. This is a good way to focus in on what's truly important to you - often we make ourselves huge lists of what we "should" be doing, and get overwhelmed by everything we then need to do to make that happen. This overwhelm can then hold us back from doing anything at all! Stripping it back to just four goals reduces that weight of expectation and shows us what really matters - all the rest is secondary.

Once you have your four goals, think about a common theme or idea that ties them all together. How do the four aims relate to one another? Where do they connect within you? Write that common theme in the thumb space on the image.

Keep this image to refer back to regularly to remind you of what's important to you and see whether you are focusing on your true priorities.

Take it further

If you want to extend this exercise, you could cover your hand in paint and use that to make the handprint on the paper. Once the paint is dry, use a coloured pen (of a colour that will show up on the paint) to draw images that represent each of your goals in the fingers, and one to represent your theme in the thumb.

14

Burst the Balloon

What you need:

- A balloon
- A marker pen or felt tip
- A pin or something sharp

Often we let our problems, our frustrations and our resentments build up in our mind until they are much bigger than they need to be. They crowd our brains and feel all-consuming. This exercise is a way of telling our brains it's ok to release these thoughts and let them disperse.

Exercise

Blow up a balloon and tie the end.

Using the marker pen or felt tip, write words and/or draw images that represent the negative emotions you want to let go of. They can all be around one particular issue or experience that has been playing on your mind, or they can be a general assortment of worries.

Once you feel you've got all of the troubling thoughts out of your brain and onto the balloon, take your pin or sharp object (please **be careful**) and take a few deep breaths. Visualise these worries filling up the balloon and swelling in the same way the balloon swelled when you filled it with air. Imagine that these thoughts have moved from your mind and are now swirling around inside the balloon instead.

Burst the balloon.

Imagine that the difficult thoughts have burst with it, and dissipated into the air.

15

Bake a Gift

What you need:

- A recipe for baked goods (make it as simple or as complicated as you like, but make sure its main ingredient is in
  season right now)
- The ingredients the recipe requires
- Any equipment the recipe calls for

Making food with your hands is deeply satisfying. It engages
all your senses, and gives you a deep sense of accomplishment
when you have the nourishing finished product. It's even more
satisfying to bake with items that you've picked yourself! I love
baking with seasonal produce because it helps me to be in tune
with the world around me. If you can't get out and forage for
food, you can buy from local markets. If you are going to pick
things yourself, make sure you know what you're doing and
consult reputable guides - some edible plants can look very

similar to poisonous ones! If you're not confident that you can tell the difference, buy it instead.

Exercise

Bake something. A pie, a cake, cookies, muffins... anything that takes your fancy. Make it using produce that is in season and, preferably, from your local area.

Give your finished product to someone as a gift. You could give it to a friend or family member, or you could donate it – there are charities that will take food to distribute to people who need it (they often need a list of ingredients, so write down everything you have put into your bake), and there are also apps that allow you to offer food to people nearby who can collect it from you.

Not only do you have the satisfaction of making something from scratch and feeling connected to the environment it came from, you also have the joy of sharing the love and energy you put into it with someone else, giving you a deeper connection with your world and your human family.

16

Relationship Target

What you need:

- Paper
- A pencil

They say you are the average of the five people you spend the most time with. Whether you agree with this or not (and it's a controversial theory), the people you give your time and energy to certainly have a big impact on you. Not only that, but we often feel compelled to spend time with people we feel we should, leaving us less time for the people we really *want* to be with. Sometimes we give certain people an unnecessary amount of power in our lives because we feel we *ought* to give them a large share of our attention or energy even though the relationship isn't benefiting us.

This exercise is a great way to help us get clear on the relationships that truly matter to us and that nourish us. Those relationships are our priority. When we identify which relationships don't bring as much positivity to our lives, we can give ourselves permission to give them a little less energy. We don't have to cut those people out of our lives, and we might not even be able to substantially reduce the time we spend with the person - this can be particularly difficult if the relationship in question is with a family member - but we can allow ourselves to invest a little less energy and attention in that relationship, giving ourself a little mental space from the person and recognising that spending time with them might be a thing we have to do but isn't something that has to matter to us or influence us.

Exercise

Draw four concentric circles (like a target image) - the smallest circle in the centre, a wider circle around it, then a wider circle around that, then a wider circle around that.

In the central circle, write the names of the people who matter the most to you. These are the people that you *love* spending time with. The people that make you feel seen and valued and uplifted when you are with them. The people who you miss when you're away from them. It's likely that there won't be many names in that circle, and that's ok - you can't expect to feel that way about many people. Don't push yourself to put names in there that you think *should* be in there. Be honest with yourself. Remember, no one else is going to see this.

In the next circle, write the names of people who enrich your life. People who bring a positive influence, whether that's giving wise advice, supporting you on your journey, or making you feel more joyful and uplifted.

In the next circle, write the names of people you like. People that you have fun with, that you enjoy spending time with, but that you don't necessarily mind going long periods of time without seeing. These are probably the people you'll have a laugh with in a pub or a cafe, people you have shared interests with that will join you for an activity, people that you wouldn't necessarily seek out but you'd be pleased to bump into.

In the final circle, write the names of people that you have relationships with but you don't particularly feel a connection to. These are likely to be the people that you feel connected to more by obligation than anything else. It could be a boss or a colleague, a friend or relative of your partner... it could even be your own parent or sibling. If you realise that a family member belongs in this outer circle, that might bring up some challenging feelings. Remember to go back to your breath, and don't pass judgement on yourself or anyone else. We're not here to judge, this is what it is - we're just observing your feelings about your relationships here. Putting their name down in this circle doesn't actually change your relationship to them, it just allows you to recognise it, honestly, for what it is.

You might find that there are people in your life that don't fit into any of those circles - people that you just don't like and don't want to spend any time with, and that you don't even feel *obligated* to spend time with. Feel free to write them down around the edges of the paper outside the outermost circle. Again, notice any feelings that come up, but don't judge the feelings or yourself. Try not to judge the person, either. They are who they are, and maybe they're just not for you.

Now you have your circles, you can take an inventory of where you spend your time. Are you prioritising those innermost relationships, or is your time being sucked up by people in that outer circle? What can you do to shift the balance and make more time - or at least more *quality* time - for the people that matter?

It's easy for people in the second and third circles to get lost in the scheduling shuffle - what can you do to proactively schedule more time with the people in your second circle? Do you need to cut down on time spent with people in the third circle to free up space, and allow time with them to happen when it happens, knowing that you won't be missing anything if you see them less?

Can you reduce time spent with people in the fourth circle? Or at least claim back some of the mental energy and headspace they're taking up? By recognising that they belong in that outer circle, you can limit some of the power they have in your mind and reduce them to the right size in your thought priorities.

The people who fall outside the circles altogether are probably people you can safely cut out of your life. It can be strange to realise we've been voluntarily spending time with people we don't like and that don't bring anything positive to our lives, but we easily fall into these habits that can seem hard to break. Once we acknowledge that these aren't our people - or that they're no longer right for this season of our life - we can consciously detach from them and allow them to fade away.

17

A Brick in the Wall

What you need:

You can keep this as simple or get as creative as you want. You could use:

- A pencil and paper
- OR modelling clay / play dough
- OR cardboard boxes
- OR pebbles (I live right next to a beach so I have a huge supply of pebbles on hand at all times)
- OR anything you can think of that you can use to make a model

We all put walls up to protect ourselves. Life can be brutal, and our hearts get bruised a fair few times as we grow. By the time we reach adulthood, we've already created a few (or many) barriers to keep the world at a distance. Sometimes these are helpful, but sometimes they can isolate us. In this exercise, we're going to take a look at these walls and where they come from so we can consciously consider what we want to keep and what we want to take down.

Exercise

Think about walls you've put up. These might include a wall between you and other people (maybe specific people, maybe just people in general), a wall you've used to cut yourself off from future experiences, or a wall you've put around your heart or your memory. You might choose to focus in on one or two specific walls, or think more generally about the barriers between you and the world around you.

Draw or build your wall. You could also represent what you're trying to keep out, or just the wall itself, it's up to you.

Now think about what the bricks are made of – what have you, metaphorically, used to construct this wall? Maybe you retreat into work, maybe you keep people away with a short temper, maybe you use humour to deflect serious talk, maybe you date multiple people at a time to keep from getting attached to one person. You could represent these "materials" in your drawing or model if you want. For example, if you've drawn a wall, you could write the words on individual bricks. If you've made a wall out of pebbles, you could use a pen to draw an image to represent the ideas on each one. Get as creative as you like.

Consider what's on the other side of the wall. What are you keeping out? What would happen if you took some of the bricks away? Are the bricks serving you? Are there more constructive materials you could use to shape a new barrier? Could that new barrier be more flexible?

You can either represent these thoughts within your drawing or model (or make a new drawing or model) or simply journal on them.

18

Childhood Memories

What you need:

- Something to write with
- Something to write on

We're going to be reflecting on our earliest memories and considering them in the light of who we are now. **This can be an uncomfortable topic.** Only you know whether you are able to safely explore your early childhood or not. It might be that it's uncomfortable, but beneficial in processing difficult experiences. However, if it's likely to be traumatic, don't do it. Instead, think back to your earliest **joyful** memories, or your happiest memories. If anything distressing does come up, please seek support from a mental health professional.

Exercise

Make a list of early memories from your childhood. Push yourself to go further and further back to see what are the earliest memories you can recall. Once you've noted down a list, see if you can put them in chronological order.

Choose two or three memories from your list (preferably the earliest ones) and write about them in more detail. Start with the words "I remember" and then note down as much sensory detail as you can recall - what can you see, hear, smell, taste, touch in that memory? What feelings does it bring back?

Now read over the memories you have written about, and consider how the younger you in your memory relates to the person you are now. Perhaps you can see the beginnings of an interest or hobby that has become a lifelong passion, or perhaps the younger you is displaying personality traits that have become stronger over time. Or maybe the person in your memory seems completely different to the present you - how have you changed? What would the person you were then be surprised about if they saw you now?

Spend some time journaling on the link between the version of you in these early memories and the person you are now, and how you got from there to here.

19

Viking Weaving

What you need:

- A piece of cardboard (any scrap piece out of the recycling is fine)
- Scissors
- Wool / yarn

Engaging your hands in a repetitive practice is incredibly soothing for your mind, and it helps to connect your brain and body, which gives you a greater sense of wholeness and therefore of ease and calm. Repetitive actions are great mindfulness practices, where you are focused on the present and the tiny details, reducing stress and lowering your blood pressure.

Viking weaving is an ancient practice - as the name suggests, it's believed to have originated with Viking communities in Scandinavia. It's a super simple weaving practice that anyone can do (I was taught how to do it by my six-year-old child). One particularly great part is that it's impossible to go wrong – if you do make a "mistake", it won't be visible in the finished weave. I know, I've checked (all in the name of science, you understand). So you can relax completely.

Exercise

Take your piece of cardboard and cut out a circle. The circle doesn't have to be especially neat, but aim to make it about the size of the palm of your hand.

Around the edge of the circle, cut eight slits, fairly evenly spaced, and about 2cm (a bit less than 1 inch) in length. It doesn't have to be exact, you just want them to be long enough that your yarn won't fall off but not so long that they crash into the middle.

Poke a hole into the middle.

Take your wool / yarn and cut seven pieces, roughly equal in length. They can all be the same colour or a selection of colours, it's up to you.

Push your seven pieces of yarn through the hole in your cardboard. Keeping the ends together, tie a knot in all seven pieces together near the end of the threads. Pull this knot to the cardboard so that it's keeping your yarn from coming out. Now place one strand into each of the slits around the edge. You'll have one slit left empty.

With the empty slit at the top, count three slits to the left, and move that yarn to the empty slit. Move the new empty slit round to the top, and, again count three to the left and move that piece of yarn to the empty slit. And continue.

If all of this is getting a bit confusing, you can find a video tutorial as part of this free class:

https://creativefix.thinkific.com/courses/creative-wellbein
g

As you go, the end poking through the hole will get longer and longer in a woven braid. You can pull it taught from time to time to make sure it keeps moving through.

When the braid is the length you want it to be, take all the pieces of yarn out of the slits and pull them all through the hole. Tie a knot at the other end and then cut off the unwoven pieces of yarn.

You can use the finished braid as a bracelet, as a trim for clothes or cushions, or as anything you want!

20

You Cloud

What you need:

- Paper (A4 or larger works best)
- A pen / pencil (coloured pens or pencils are great if you have them, but just one regular pen or pencil works fine)

This is like a word cloud for your sense of self! A chance to think deeply about what makes you who you are, and which attributes you feel are most important, as well as which ones you want to work on.

Exercise

Write your name in the centre of the piece of paper. Draw a nice shape or outline around it. Decorate it any way you want.

Now in other bubbles / shapes (different coloured ones, if you like), write as many words or short phrases that you think are, or you would like to be, associated with you. These can be ways you see, or want to see, yourself, and/or ways you would like others to see you, words you'd like people to associate with you, ways you'd like to be remembered.

This is not a space to put yourself down - don't include any negative thoughts about yourself, even if you're totally convinced that is how other people see you (I'm pretty sure it's not, by the way). If it's a word some people might see as negative, but you see positive sides to it and it feels good to you, then you can include it. But this is a space for collecting the positive words that have value to you.

Don't overthink it, just write the words down as they come to you. Be bold!

Set a timer for 10 minutes - it helps to focus the mind.

When the 10 minutes is up and you have a variety of words on the page, consider which have the most meaning. Which do you think are the most central to who you are? Which are the ones you most want to work towards? Go over these words with your pen or pencil several times to make them bold, maybe underline them or decorate them in some way - do whatever you like to make them stand out.

Maybe there's one or two words that are the most important that you want to make stand out more than any others and decorate in a bigger way.

You could even write the whole thing out again and make the most important words the biggest, with words decreasing in size depending on their level of significance. Then you could decorate them any way you like.

This is yours to do what you want with!

21

Lesson Generator

What you need:

- Paper
- Pencil
- **Optional:** Cardboard and glue / sellotape OR modelling clay / play dough OR any other model-making materials if you're choosing to make a model
- **Optional:** paints, crayons, pastels... any art materials you want to use for decoration

Finding lessons and meaning in difficult experiences can help us to move forward from them. I'm not big on the whole "everything happens for a reason, every trauma is a gift sent to teach you something" stuff - I think, sometimes, life is just a bit sh*t for absolutely no reason. Not everything bad that happens has to have been sent by the universe with some divine meaning. But that doesn't mean that we can't still take learnings from the random crap that bumps into us. Not every time, maybe – some things really are just sh*t – but most times I think it is possible to learn something about yourself, your capabilities, the world around you or what you need/want. If you'd like to find some meaning in dark times, then you can build your own lesson generator.

Exercise

Firstly, draw your experience, or your feelings towards it. This can be as messy and chaotic as you want it to be – this is a picture of the impact this has had on you, your emotional state, your sense of yourself after the thing. You can choose to depict actual events or images that represent your experience, or you could use colours/ shapes/ patterns to express the feelings associated with it.

Now, make the lesson generator. You can draw it or make it as a model, but the lesson generator is a machine to extract learnings from experiences. Whatever that looks like to you, make it so.

Now feed your experience into the machine – you can do this literally if your machine is a model, or just in your imagination if it's a drawing. You might choose to symbolically place the drawing of your machine over the drawing of the experience.

Then draw what comes out of the machine. What lessons, meaning and/or opportunities has the machine presented you with? (If you don't want to draw the product, you could write about the lessons.)

57

22

Nothing Left Unsaid

What you need:

- Paper
- Pen

We all have situations that fester in our memories - unresolved issues or people that we feel wronged us and who never acknowledged what they did. Those resentments you think you've moved on from until, out of nowhere, you'll remember what happened and feel angry or hurt or frustrated all over again. These feelings are an inevitable part of life, but the more we allow them to take up space in our subconscious, the more they drain our energy and eat away at our joy. They can make us bitter and negative, which is bad for our health. This exercise helps to get all the difficult feelings out onto the page so that we can start to release them and move on.

Exercise

Write a letter to a person or situation that you are still angry about or resentful of. No one is going to see this letter, so don't worry about what you put into it. Get all of your feelings out onto the page. Make sure that nothing is left unsaid.

When you're done and you feel like you've said everything that has been playing on your mind about this person or situation, burn the letter. **Make sure you do this safely**, in a fireplace or fireproof dish. Alternatively, you could tear up the letter and dispose of the pieces. Visualise the hold that these feelings have had over you breaking apart and flying away as the letter burns / tears. Say goodbye to those feelings and tell yourself it's time to move forward.

23

Making Meaning

What you need:

- Paper
- Pen
- **Optional:** Pencil / crayons / pastels

One of the wonderful things about language is that each word has so many different meanings and associations. Playing with all these different levels of meaning can add richness and depth to your creative projects, and help you to explore your ideas and the different meanings and connections that you hold in your subconscious.

Exercise

Make a list of all the different meanings, interpretations or associations you can think of for the word "creation". Set a timer for three minutes and write down as many as you can think of in that time.

Choose three or four of the ideas on your list that stand out to you, and create a sketch or write a short paragraph about each one.

Then choose one of those ideas to explore further, either in a piece of writing or in another form of art.

24

Light It Up

What you need:

- Paper
- Pencil

Taking time to think about the things that bring us joy helps to activate endorphins in our brains. Imaging an experience or an activity causes a similar reaction in your brain to the real thing. This burst of "happy hormones" reduces stress, anxiety and depression, and increases positivity, resilience and cognitive function. This has a whole host of health benefits. In addition, getting clear on what lights you up allows you to consider where you're focusing your energy and what you can make space for in your life that will bring you more joy.

Exercise

Draw an image of a lightbulb - it should take up most of your piece of paper.

Inside the lightbulb shape, put things that light you up. You can represent these using words or drawings.

You can interpret "light you up" however makes sense to you - there are no right or wrong answers.

25

What Love Means

What you need:

- Paper
- Pen

We spend a lot of time thinking about big topics in our lives, often without being clear on what they truly mean to us or what we want from them. This is an opportunity to take one of those big topics and explore how you view it and how you want it to show up in your life.

Exercise

Sit somewhere fairly quiet where you won't be disturbed or interrupted.

At the top of the page, write "What does love mean to me?"

Then answer the question. Commit to writing for at least ten minutes - you might find it helpful to set a timer.

26

Mountains and Valleys

What you need:

- Paper
- Pencil
- Pen

Life is full of ups and downs. Often the downs can feel more urgent and therefore take up a lot more of our headspace, leading to mental and physical health issues. But trying to focus exclusively on the ups doesn't help, either. You can't deny reality, and trying to do so isn't good for you. We have to be able to look at all of life as it is.

Looking back over a period of time - the last three months, six months, the year that's just gone - and reflecting on the highs and the lows can give us perspective. It helps us to appreciate the moments of joy and achievement, and to acknowledge and process the struggles and challenges. We can also look back with pride, not only on what we've accomplished, but also what we've overcome.

This is a great exercise to do on New Year's Eve or the night before your birthday, to reflect on a year gone by, but it works any time.

Exercise

On your piece of paper, draw a snaking line that represents mountains and valleys... something like this:

The mountains represent the positive moments, the time when everything felt on the up, whereas the valleys represent the times where you felt low or where you were going through challenges.

You might feel that, across the time period that you're looking at, there were clearly defined "high" and "low" periods, in which case you could do this chronologically. Or you may have had more of a mixture of highs and lows all in the mix together - in that case, you may want to group related ups and downs together, using whatever theme feels right to you.

There is no "correct" way to do this, it is simply a way to reflect on your experiences over time.

Now, on each mountain, list the positive events, experiences and emotions of the time period that this space represents to you. You might want to write a little about each one, or you might want to draw images to express what took place and how you feel about that time. In the valleys, do the same for the more challenging times and experiences.

You can add photos, mementos, drawings, poems or anything else that expresses your feelings or captures key memories about those times to the relevant mountains and valleys if you wish.

Now look back over everything you experienced in this time-frame. Think about what you have taken away from this time, what lessons you've gained, as well as what you can take forward with you into the future and what you'd prefer to leave behind. Take a moment to express gratitude for the gifts of that time, and to congratulate yourself for everything you've achieved and overcome.

27

Musical Visualisation

What you need:

- Instrumental music (if you don't own any yourself, go to YouTube, Spotify or any music streaming service of your choice and search for instrumental music – any genre is fine; you could choose something you know you like, or challenge yourself to listen to something a bit out of your comfort zone!)
- Paper
- Pen / pencil / crayons

Music is seriously good for your health. Studies have found that it helps to improve cognitive function and memory, reduce anxiety and blood pressure, relieve pain and improve sleep quality, boost mood and increase alertness. This exercise allows you to fully engage with the music.

Exercise

You will want to be somewhere quiet where you won't be disturbed and you will feel safe and secure. Keep your paper and pen/pencil and/or other art materials close by. Put on your chosen piece of music and sit or lie down with your eyes closed. Just listen to the music.

Allow different images, shapes, colours and ideas to come to you as you listen. Don't judge any thoughts that come up, and don't try to direct your mind. Simply allow your brain to respond to the music.

When the piece has finished, open your eyes, and draw or write about what you saw. If it was predominantly shapes and colours, then represent those on the page in as abstract a way as you like. If a defined story came to you, write it down.

Take it further

To extend this exercise, you could then paint the images/colours you saw, or create a collage with different materials and textures to represent the experience of the music.

28

Nature Collage

What you need:

- Paper
- Glue and/or sellotape

Time in nature has huge benefits for physical and mental health, so combining it with creativity can only be a good thing! Working with nature in your creativity also helps to build an appreciation for, and connection to, the world around you. For this exercise, you will ideally want to head to a natural space, like the woods, fields, a beach... anywhere there is an abundance of nature. But if that's tricky, whatever outdoor space you can easily access will almost certainly have what you need.

Exercise

Head out to your chosen outdoor space, and look around for beautiful things that catch your eye. Flowers, pebbles, twigs, leaves, grass, sand, shells... whatever you like. Collect the items that you want to take home with you, providing that it is safe and responsible to do so (mostly you won't come into any issues, but it can be harmful or even illegal to pick certain wildflowers, and some plants may be poisonous, so check before taking anything you're unsure of).

When you get home, create a collage or display. This might involve sticking your items onto a piece of paper or, if you have larger items (such as pebbles), you could arrange them in a dish or tray, or create a picture or pattern with them in your garden.

You could paint or decorate your items, or introduce paint or other collage materials to your paper amongst the nature items.

Have fun with this in any way you like.

29

Power Pose

What you need:

- Paper
- Pencil

Today is the day to engage in some serious pumping yourself up. Us humans are pretty good at constantly telling ourselves our own flaws and weaknesses, but how often do you celebrate the *truly awesome* stuff about yourself? ... Yeah, that's what I thought. Well, the time has come.

Exercise

Draw yourself. Depending on how good you feel about drawing, this can be an actual picture of yourself, or a stick figure, or something in between. But it should be a whole body.

Next to each of the different parts or areas of your body (or as many as you can), write something that you are proud of it for, or an achievement it has brought you. This could include things like hands that are good at painting, legs that have run a marathon or a heart that gives love to your family. You can be as literal or as metaphorical as you like. You don't have to focus on things you're "good" at – things you enjoy just for the sake of them are totally valid too.

30

Expressing Admiration

What you need:

- Paper
- Pen
- Pencil
- **Optional:** Internet connection and printer

We live in a highly individualistic world that puts a lot of pressure on us to be the stars of our own shows. Whilst it's great to celebrate our abilities and successes, we also benefit a lot from celebrating other people and appreciating the people that we admire. We can also consider what it is about them that we admire and what traits we might therefore like to cultivate more in ourselves.

Exercise

Make a list of people that you admire. What "admiration" means here is entirely up to you.

Next, find or draw images of them, or create images that in some way represent them to you. If you're finding images online, print them out.

Alongside each image, write down the qualities that you admire in that person.

31

Box of You

What you need:

- Paper bag / cardboard box
- Crayons / pastels / pencils
- Glue / sellotape

Understanding who you are as a person is the work of a lifetime. The more we try to recognise who we are, the more we can live authentically in a way that focuses on what matters to us. Spending time thinking about who we are and what shapes us also helps us to foster self-compassion and to treat ourselves more kindly and gently.

Exercise

Take a paper bag or a cardboard box, and decorate it with images that represent you. You could draw a picture of yourself, or draw/stick on pictures of things that matter to you or represent aspects of your personality.

Over the next week, collect images, quotes, photographs, pieces of your own writing, your own sketches/doodles, and anything else that represents who you are and what matters to you - add them to the bag/box.

At the end of the week, take everything out of the bag/box and turn it into a collage.

Reflect on what that collage says about you, and about your needs and wants.

32

Free Writing

What you need:

- Pen
- Paper

"Free writing" is also sometimes called "stream of conscious-ness" writing. The idea is to constantly keep your pen moving, even if you keep writing "I don't know what to write, I don't know what to write" until your brain comes up with something to write. Eventually, your subconscious will kick in and supply some words. Your job is just to keep the ink flowing and allow your mind to pour thoughts out onto the page. It's a great exercise for letting out all that noise that has been swirling around your brain, and also for uncovering how you truly feel about issues that you might feel confused or conflicted about. Once you start writing, you find your deeper feelings come out.

Exercise

Set a timer for 10 minutes so that you won't be tempted to keep checking how long you've been writing for and you can commit yourself to continually writing for the full amount of time. Then start writing and keep going until the timer goes off, in response to the following question (write the question at the top of the page, if you like, to get you started):

What am I waiting for?

33

Fresh Eyes

What you need:

- A camera (a smartphone is fine)
- Paper
- Pen

This exercise challenges you to look closely, working on the mindfulness benefits that we discussed earlier. By paying careful attention to somewhere that you know so well that you have stopped really noticing it, you stimulate the creative and visual part of your brain, and learn to look at the world with a greater level of awareness and appreciation.

Exercise

Visit a place you know well, but where you don't live - it could be a family member's home, a cafe you go to all the time, or a public place you spend a lot of time in. Try to see the place with fresh eyes - what small details do you notice? How would someone experience this place coming here for the first time? What sounds, smells, sensations would they experience? Take photos of little details, or from angles you don't normally look from.

Afterwards, journal about what you noticed, and what the experience would be like for someone totally new to that space.

34

Life Compass

What you need:

- Paper
- Pen / pencil

Sometimes, we need to find a sense of direction in life. It's easy to feel lost in all the chaos and busyness and lose sight of what matters or where we want to go. This exercise is a way to focus on your personal inner compass.

Exercise

Draw a basic compass shape in the middle of your paper, leaving plenty of space around the outside of your shape. Something like this:

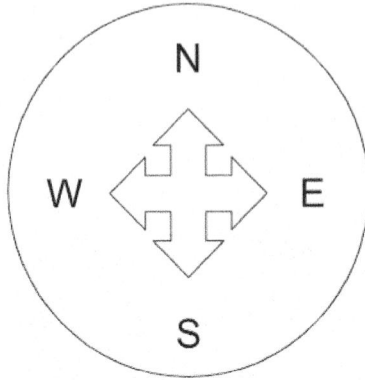

- Above the North point, write down one word or a very short sentence for each of the things that really matter to you – the very most important elements of your life. These are your true north.
- Next to the East point, write down all the things you have to do, all the elements in your life that are necessary, but that don't actually mean that much to you.
- Next to the West point, write down all the things you enjoy doing, all the elements of life that are fun and pleasant, but that don't feel particularly essential or meaningful.
- Below the South point, write down all the elements of your life that you would like to leave behind.

If you prefer to use images to represent each element, or a mixture of images and words, go for it. Whatever feels right to you is the right thing to do.

35

In the Picture

What you need:

- Access to an artwork, either in a gallery or online
- Pen
- Paper

Taking time to engage with different forms of art not only gives you all the health benefits we've already talked about, but it helps to unlock your imagination and encourage greater creativity within yourself. The more you immerse yourself in other people's art, the more you'll be inspired to create your own - and you already know how good that is for you!

Exercise

Go to an art gallery and look at a painting. If that's impossible, find an artwork online.

You might find it easier to use a painting that depicts a real person or scene, but it's not essential. If you want to stretch yourself, you can use abstract art.

Imagine what is going on in the painting. If there is a person, or people, in it, what are they thinking or feeling? What's just happened? What will happen next?

Now write about it.

36

Happy Place

What you need:

- Photos or a printer
- Paper
- Glue
- Scissors
- **Optional:** paint, pastels, crayons, or other art materials

This is not only a great way to release some endorphins in your brain and immerse yourself in some creative wellbeing, but it's an opportunity to create a piece of art that you can look at whenever you need a lift.

Exercise

Find or print out some photos of scenes, people, activities, objects, places or anything else that symbolise "happiness" to you.

Once again, it's not about what you think "should" make you happy, or about anyone else's idea of happiness. This is about what speaks to you.

Use these photos to make a collage - stick them onto the paper in any arrangement that feels good.

You can decorate your collage with other art materials if you wish to.

37

Spotting Colour

What you need:

· A camera (a smartphone is fine)

This is another mindfulness exercise, designed to help you pay close attention to the world around you, and to notice how magical and colourful it really is!

Exercise

Choose a colour. Any colour you like.

Now go outside. (If it's really not an option to go out, you can do this exercise around your home, but I encourage you to get outdoors if you possibly can.) Take photos of as many things as you can find that are your chosen colour.

Take it further

If you want to extend this exercise, when you get back home, print out the photos you took and make a collage with them.

38

Mind Map

What you need:

- Paper
- Pen
- **Optional:** Coloured pens / pencils

You probably made mind maps at school, where you start with one central word and then write words around it that you associate with that original word. Then around each of the new words, write words you associate with *that* word. And so on. The idea is to explore layers of meaning and connection. When you look at how different concepts relate to one another, you can discover links that you hadn't thought of before - and that can be hugely beneficial for your creativity. This exercise can also help you to look at a particular topic in new ways and find new perspectives or deeper levels of understanding.

Exercise

In the centre of your paper, draw a circle and write the word "history".

Around that word, draw more circles (or a different shape), and in each of those write different words that you associate with the word history. Then repeat the process with each new word.

Keep going until you have lots of levels of words. Then look over your mind map and identify any interesting trends or connections that reveal themselves.

Take it further

To extend this exercise, choose a selection of words that form an interesting connection, or a word that you feel is surprising in its link to "history" and use that concept as the starting point for a piece of writing or art.

39

Remember You

What you need:

- Pen
- Paper

We get so caught up in the day-to-day that life can feel like it's whizzing by, like the view from a train window. Rather than let time run away with us, it does us good to sit and reflect on what we want our lives to look like. If we don't know what we want, we can't consciously work towards it. And then we find ourselves eaten up by bitterness and resentment when we sense that other people have something we wanted, even if we can't quite name it. So name it now, then walk towards it.

Exercise

We are *many* years into the future, and you are being profiled in a magazine, very late in your life. The article is looking back over your life and celebrating all that you have done. Perhaps you have been given a lifetime achievement award for a particular body of work or contribution to society, or perhaps it is a human interest piece celebrating a colourful life well lived.

Write that article.

As part of that process, consider what you want to be remembered for, and what you would like to look back on when you approach the end of your life.

40

Seasonal Sensations

What you need:

- Pen
- Paper

By now, I'm sure I've repeated quite enough how many benefits there are to mindfulness, and to connecting to the natural world. So I won't repeat myself about how taking time to pay attention to the world around you helps reduce stress and anxiety, as well as lowering your blood pressure, or how spending time in nature improves your mental and physical health. Or maybe just one more time.

Here, we're going to be using mindfulness to observe the changing seasons and recognise how the world around us shifts over time.

Exercise

Start by writing the name of the season you are currently in at the top of your page.

Now make five columns, and write the following words at the top:

1. Sight
2. Smell
3. Touch
4. Taste
5. Sound

In each column, write as many things as you can think of that relate to that sense that you associate with this season. Don't overthink it, and don't feel you need to justify your choices, just scribble down as many things as you can think of that feel relevant for **any** reason. You might find it helpful to set a timer for five minutes to force you to focus on getting as many things down as you can and then to let go.

Once you have your column lists, choose one item from each column. Again, don't think too much about it, just look down each column and circle the item that calls to you or jumps out at you.

Then, set a timer for ten minutes and write a piece - fiction or non-fiction - that incorporates those five things.

41

Dear Me

What you need:

- Pen
- Paper

We can often be much better at saying kind and loving things to others than we are to ourselves. Instead, our "inner critic" encourages us to say things to ourselves that we would never *dream* of saying to anyone else. Time to take a break from being hard on yourself and show yourself some love.

Exercise

Write a love letter to yourself.

Think about what you would say if you were writing a love letter to someone else - you would tell them all the things you think are amazing about them, maybe tell them how proud or impressed you are by their achievements, you might reminisce about great times you've had together, you would probably talk about things you are looking forward to sharing with them in the future. Do all of that, but for yourself.

This may well feel *incredibly* uncomfortable at first, and you may feel yourself resisting it. You will probably want to hold back in the language that you use.

I encourage you to push through that discomfort. Recognise any resistance you're experiencing, and be curious about where that's coming from. But keep going. Invite yourself to be as mushy and soppy as you can. Challenge yourself to be absolutely over-the-top gushing about how amazing you are. Once you get into it, it will start to feel easier.

Take it further

You could post the letter to yourself, then save it somewhere hidden. When you feel down and need a lift, open the letter and read how incredible you truly are.

42

Memory Bag

What you need:

- Paper bag OR cardboard box OR any container you like
- Paper
- Pen / pencil
- **Optional:** Crayons, paint, pastels, and any other materials you'd like to use

Often we hold onto difficult memories, even when we want to let them go. We replay them again and again, which basically means we're reliving them and our bodies are experiencing, over and over, the increased cortisol that comes with stress, which is bad for our health. Sorting through the memory bag can be a good way to become more aware of what we're hanging on to, and make a conscious effort to let some of it go.

Exercise

Take your paper bag or chosen container. If you like, you can decorate the outside with drawings, words or collage items that represent you.

Then, on small pieces of paper, draw/write images, words or phrases to represent the memories that are strongest in your mind, or that you are aware most often come up in your mind. These could be happy memories, or they could be difficult ones. You will most likely end up with a mixture of both, and a fair few that have a variety of emotions associated with them.

You could choose to cover an entire period of time - for example, if something challenging happened when you were a young child, you could make memories, good and bad, that you have from your childhood before the age of 10. Or you could focus in on a particular situation or person - for example, if you're processing a difficult experience or relationship, you could depict memories specifically related to that situation or person. It's entirely up to you.

Only you know what you are able to work with. If a particular topic is too distressing, please don't use it for this exercise. There is a line between difficult experiences that you will benefit from working through using creative methods, and experiences that are too traumatic to revisit without professional support. You are the only person who can judge what's appropriate for you. If you get into the exercise and realise a topic is too triggering after all, feel free to step away from it and either choose something else or end the exercise altogether.

Put all of the memories you create into the bag, and shake it up. Go and make a cup of tea, have a bath, go for a walk - do something to calm your mind and give yourself a breather.

Come back to the bag when you're ready.

Take out the memories one at a time, and reflect on what this signifies to you and why you're holding onto it. You might choose to do some drawing or painting to express these thoughts, or journal on them. You can pace yourself with this task - if there are a lot of memories, or if you're finding them painful to think about, you don't have to do them all in one go.

Once the bag is empty, look at the memories and consider what you want to keep, and what you'd like to let go of. There's no right or wrong answers to this - it's not as simple as "get rid of the bad memories, keep the good ones". Some memories will contain both joy and grief. Some might be painful, but you choose to keep them because they've given you valuable lessons or brought you to a positive place in the long term. Whatever memories you feel are right for you to keep, put back in the bag. Any that you don't feel are serving you or that you want to let go of, leave out. You can throw these away, burn them, or turn them into another piece of art.

43

The Other Side of the Story

What you need:

- Pen
- Paper

It's easy to get stuck in our own heads and think that our way of thinking is the right one. We tend to spend a lot of our time - both online and offline - in echo chambers with people who share our views, which reinforces this idea that everyone who disagrees is evil and/or stupid. The trouble with this way of thinking is that it fills us full of rage and bitterness, and creates divides in our society. We're becoming more and more polarised, and unable to have meaningful conversations with people we disagree with. Which means everyone is becoming more entrenched in their own viewpoints and unwilling to hear differing opinions, so no one will ever change their mind and we'll never be able to move forward. It's not healthy, and it's not workable.

Building skills in empathy and compassion, and being able to see things from other perspectives, helps us to feel more positive about the world, be kinder to others, and listen more effectively. We don't have to agree with what we're hearing, but we can be compassionate towards the person saying it. If we understand their concerns, we might even be better able to show them our own point of view. At the very least, we'll feel better and we'll be putting more positivity and kindness out into the world.

Exercise

Choose a topic that you have a strong opinion about.

Now write a speech passionately arguing in favour of the *opposite* opinion.

It's best not to choose something that is going to trigger you personally - leave things that relate to your own identity or experience. Avoid identity altogether - you don't want to find yourself arguing against someone's existence. Although most strong opinions will have impact on people's lives, so be prepared to potentially face some tough issues.

Try to see the topic from the other "side's" point of view. You might vehemently disagree with them and see huge problems with where their thinking leads, but you can try to empathise with the fears, concerns, misunderstandings, experiences or societal messages that have led them in this direction.

By putting yourself in another person's shoes, you open yourself up to recognising that yours isn't the only way to see the world.

Now that you know what someone who disagrees with you is worried about or looking for, try writing a speech that argues in favour of your original point of view, but in a way that addresses their concerns, speaks to them with empathy and respect and looks for solutions that will allow you both to move forward.

44

A Picture Paints a Thousand Words

What you need:

- A book (fiction or narrative non-fiction)
- Paper (A4 or larger)
- Coloured pencils / pastels / paints / any materials you like

In a previous exercise, we wrote about a painting in order to immerse ourselves in someone else's work and stimulate our own creativity. In this exercise, we're going to do the same but in reverse!

Exercise

Choose a book that you love, or that's about a topic you're really interested in. Either pick one you own at home, or take a trip to a library.

Read an extract from that book – if you know it well, you might be able to easily find a passage you enjoy, or you could just open it at a random page and read a few paragraphs. You might like to read the extract a few times to get it clear in your mind.

Then create an image to represent that extract. It could be a realistic depiction of the scene or person described, or it could be an abstract expression of the emotions or ideas. It's entirely up to you.

45

The Ones I Love

What you need:

- Paper
- Pencil
- Pen

This is another exercise that you can use to create an artwork that you can look back on when you need an emotional boost, and to remind you of what really matters in life.

Exercise

Draw a large heart shape on your piece of paper.

Within that shape, write the names of each of the people / animals / places / objects / activities that you love (leave plenty of space around each name).

Next to each name, write a sentence or two, or draw a picture, expressing why you love them.

46

Getting Grounded

What you need:

- Access to nature
- Pen / pencil
- Paper

We spend a lot of time in our heads, and that can be stressful. We're either worrying about the future or ruminating on the past, and both those activities are bad for our wellbeing. Spending some time being in our bodies, noticing what we experience through our senses in the here and now, and connecting to the world around us has huge benefits for our mental and physical health, leaving us more relaxed, increasing our resilience and boosting our immunity.

Exercise

Head out into nature. A forest, a meadow, a beach... preferably somewhere that you are away from man-made noises and where there aren't too many people. Make sure, though, that it is somewhere safe and that you take any necessary precautions.

Sit somewhere you feel comfortable. If it feels safe to do so, close your eyes; otherwise, simply soften your gaze. What can you hear? Smell? Feel? Concentrate on the information your senses are giving you. Don't judge that information - it doesn't have to be "good" or "bad", it just is. Just notice it. Do this for as long as you can - you might like to set a timer in order to push yourself to stay still for 10 / 15 minutes, or even longer if possible.

When your time is up, open your eyes and then write about what you experienced, or draw images to represent your sensations.

47

Doodle Squares

What you need:

- Paper
- Pencil

If your teacher at school told you to stop doodling because it was distracting, they weren't completely correct. Doodling actually improves focus, and can help prevent your mind from wandering. It can help you recall information and support your brain in making connections and unlocking insights. It has also been shown to help reduce stress, increase blood flow to the brain and improve memory, as well as enabling you to uncover thoughts and feelings to allow you to process and balance your emotions. So don't stop doodling.

Exercise

Draw a simple 3x3 grid, a little like this:

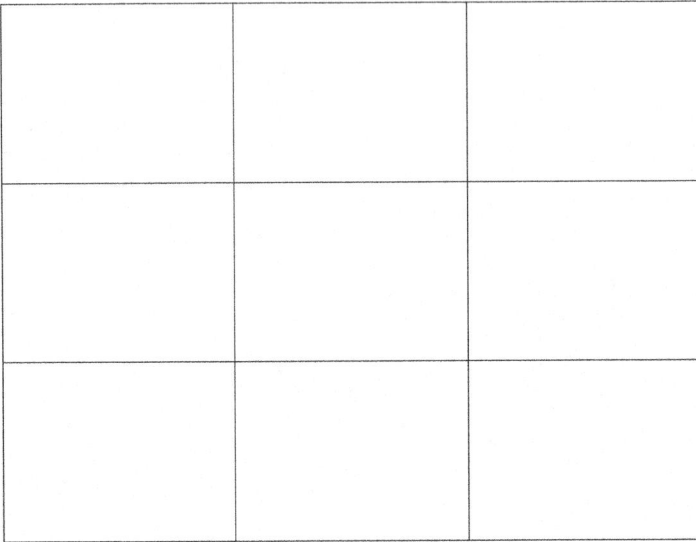

In each box, doodle. But use each box in a different way - use different patterns, lines or shapes. The idea is not to try to draw anything in particular, but just to make repetitive movements. Don't think too much about it, just let your pencil flow.

48

Common Scents

What you need:

- Pen
- Paper
- **Optional:** Crayons / pencils / paints / pastels / any art materials you like

A lot of creative work tends to focus on sight - we create visual images, or we write about the world we see around us. We also use our hearing if we're taking ideas from something we've listened to, or if we're writing dialogue. But we tend to neglect our other senses, and yet all of them work closely together. And smell can be an incredibly powerful way to access memories and explore emotions.

Exercise

Go to a shop that has a number of different scents – it could be perfumes, or scented candles, maybe bath products, anything as long as there's a good variety. It doesn't have to be anywhere fancy – I have spent considerable amounts of time amongst the scented candles in supermarkets before now, so this really can be done anywhere!

Take your time inhaling the different smells.

Pay attention to whether any particular fragrances evoke certain memories, emotions or associations in you. For example, the smell of baked apples will always take me back to my grandmother's kitchen, and the amber and leather candle I tried today immediately made me think of obnoxious men in suits.

Journal on what comes up for you. Alternatively, you could create a drawing or painting to express it.

49

Love Jar

What you need:

- A jar (or some kind of container)
- Paper
- Pen

We've already talked about the fact that it's easier to focus on the negative than the positive, and this can become overwhelming. By making an effort to consciously look for the good, we lift our mood, become more relaxed, reduce our blood pressure, and can even boost our immune systems and reduce inflammation. Here we're not just noticing positive things, we're storing them away so that we can remind ourselves when we need a lift.

Exercise

Take your jar or container. You can decorate it if you like, then put it somewhere you can easily access it every day. Keep some small pieces, or scraps, of paper nearby, along with a pen or pencil.

Every time someone makes you feel loved or cared about, write it down on a piece of paper and add it to the jar.

When the jar is full, or when you're feeling down or stressed, look through the notes in your jar.

Take it further

When the jar is full and needs to be emptied, you could use the notes to make a collage, or to inspire an artwork or piece of writing.

Then start filling the jar up again with new notes.

50

Moving On

What you need:

- Paper (some for taking notes, some for writing or drawing)
- Pen OR pencils / crayons / other art materials

Playing with different associations and images helps to stimulate your creativity and unleash your imagination. Exploring different ideas encourages you to be more playful and experimental, without any pressure, and allowing yourself to relax into the creative act.

Exercise:

Write down as many examples of "movement" as you can think of.

These can be literal or figurative, and can have as tenuous a link as you like. No one's going to be judging your list, there are no right or wrong answers.

If you're struggling, here are a few to get you started:

- A bird in flight
- A child running
- The waves breaking on the shore

Now choose one item from your list as a prompt for a piece of writing or drawing/ painting.

51

Photo Shopping

What you need:

- Old photos (of people you don't know)
- Pen
- Paper

Imagining other lives and ways of being increases empathy and compassion, as well as helping us to build better relationships with the real life people around us. It also allows us to put our own experiences into perspective, recognising that we're not alone in what we're feeling or going through - even as times change, the ups and downs, the needs and concerns are largely universal.

Exercice

Find some old photos - the older the better. These should be of people you don't know - don't choose family photos. You might be able to find some in a charity shop, or you can just search online for black and white photographs.

Look at the people in the pictures, and imagine what their lives might be like. What do they care about? What do they want? What makes them happy? What do they worry about? What does their day-to-day look like? What's on their mind while they're having their photo taken? What were they doing right before? What will they do next?

Choose one of the people you've been looking at, and write a diary entry from their point of view.

52

Pattern Matching

What you need:

- Pen
- Paper (one piece of any size, just for taking notes, and one piece of A4 or larger)
- Pencil / crayons / charcoal / pastels / paints / any art materials you like

Now that you've spent a lot of time reflecting on who you are and what is meaningful to you, there might be some patterns emerging. It's useful to explore and understand these patterns, as they help you better understand yourself, which can help you to better care for and nurture yourself.

Exercise

Thinking back over all the exercises you've done so far (you could look back on any notes or pictures you've created if it helps), think about any patterns or themes that you've noticed. Then try to finish each of these sentences with a single word (I will allow you two or three words in exceptional circumstances, but try to stick to one if you can).

In each case, write the whole sentence down for yourself. There's magic in setting the words down on paper!

What matters to me is _____
_____.

I want to be the type of person who is _____
_____.

I want people to see me as _____
_____.

I want to spend my life actively engaged in _____
_____.

Try to listen to your instinctive response to each prompt and put down what comes up for you rather than overthinking it. Aim to spend no more than 5 - 10 minutes finishing these sentences.

Now look at your responses and consider the themes in your work so far.

How can you express all that in one visual image?

Allow yourself to experiment with the materials you've chosen - you don't need to set out with the aim of producing a specific image, unless you want to. You can just let yourself play with your chosen medium (or media), keeping those words and themes in mind, until an image reveals itself. That image might be completely abstract - it might be more a sense of the words / themes conveyed through colour, texture, shape, or whatever works for you. Or it might be a realistic image of something in particular. There are no rights and wrongs, this is all about expressing yourself and allowing yourself to give life, energy and shape to the feelings deep inside of you.

Afterword

Thank you!

I hope you have enjoyed the exercises in this book and that you are enthusiastic about continuing a regular creative practice to support your emotional wellbeing.

If you're looking for more exercises and a way to dive deeper with using creativity to understand and express your emotions, join us in The Gathering on Substack. You'll find regular creative prompts, monthly workshops to access on your own schedule, regular live online sessions, a supportive creative community, and my weekly blogs.

You can join us at GatherTogether.Substack.com.

Never forget that you are a creative soul, and that your deepest emotions deserve expression.

Keep on creating.

About the Author

Allegra Chapman is an author and columnist, whose words have appeared in i News, The Independent, Newsweek and more. She is also the Co-Creator of Watch This Sp_ce, a multi-award-winning diversity and inclusion consultancy, and co-author of *The Inclusion Journey*, as well as a creative wellbeing practitioner. In 2023, she was named by f:Entrepreneur as one of the most inspirational female entrepreneurs in the UK. Allegra lives on the south coast of England with her husband and two children.

You can connect with me on:
- https://gathertogether.substack.com
- https://www.threads.net/allegra__chapman
- https://instagram.com/allegra__chapman

Printed in Dunstable, United Kingdom